Filled with Joy provides life coaching services and the necessary tools to become successful personally and professionally. Filled with Joy's mission is to assist people in their wellness journey and help them reach their goals. I hope this book finds you well as you will be able to process your thoughts and feelings and most importantly self-reflect.

30
Self
Reflection
Prompts

AND POSITIVE AFFIRMATIONS

" I'm Talking Real Love " - Mary J. Blige

We Always want to love others but do you love yourself?
Tell me 7 reasons why you love yourself?

1. _______________________________
2. _______________________________
3. _______________________________
4. _______________________________
5. _______________________________
6. _______________________________
7. _______________________________

WERE YOU ABLE TO WRITE 7 REASONS WHY? YES OR NO WRITE DOWN YOUR THOUGHTS?

____
____
____
____
____
____
____
____
____
____
____
____
____

Focus on what's strong and not wrong

Easy for us to focus on what's not going right in our lives. I do not have this, I can't do that...

Write down 10 things you are grateful for

1.__________________________
2.__________________________
3.__________________________
4.__________________________
5.__________________________
6.__________________________
7.__________________________
8.__________________________
9.__________________________
10.__________________________

WRITE DOWN YOUR THOUGHTS?

Nothing will make you happy until you choose happiness

What are some things that make you happy? Can you name at least 10 things? **Yes or NO**

What are some steps you can take to sustain happiness ?

I am worthy and I am worth it

Self Compassion

Sometimes we are nicer to others than ourselves

List some things you told yourself about yourself?

Were they nice things? If not, let's replace them with kinder thoughts

---

"Self Compassion is nurturing yourself with all the kindness and love you would shower someone you cherish" - Debra L. Reble, PHD

Be Honest
Be Gentle
Be Kind

To yourself

Negative Expectancy

We speak negatives into our lives. I can't get this job, I can't get out of debt, I will never get married. These are negative thoughts that you speak into reality. What are some negative thoughts you spoke of? What can you say differently?

Let's Journal

Lets check in on your thoughts and feelings. Give yourself time to reflect on the last few prompts and reflect on your day.

Good luck on your self reflection journey

"Time spent in self-reflection is
never wasted, it is an intimate date with
yourself"

-Paul TP Wong

If you can change one thing about your past, what would it be and why?

"If you don't like something, change it. If you can't change it, change your attitude" - Maya Angelou

What would you like to change about yourself?
Example- I would like to change how I react to things because I am in control of me

____
____
____
____
____
____
____
____
____
____
____
____

Now that you are aware, lets make some changes

9

I am the best version of myself? True or False
If true- write 10 reasons why
If false- write 10 ways you can become a better you

1. _______________________________________
2. _______________________________________
3. _______________________________________
4. _______________________________________
5. _______________________________________
6. _______________________________________
7. _______________________________________
8. _______________________________________
9. _______________________________________
10. _______________________________________

WRITE DOWN YOUR THOUGHTS?

____
____
____
____
____
____
____
____
____
____
____
____

I am

enough

Count to 10

Think of a time that you wish you would have handled a situation differently. Now count to 10.

What would you have done differently?

It's ok, just practice for the next time

Mindfullness Activity

Take 5 Deep breaths. What do you see? What do your hear? What do you smell? Let's practice living in the moment. How did it feel ? Do you know how to live in the moment?

____
____
____
____
____
____
____
____
____
____
____
____
____
____
____
____
____
____
____
____
____
____
____

Where is your happy place and why?

____
____
____
____
____
____
____
____
____
____
____
____

Draw your happy place. It doesn't have to be perfect

Think of 4 colors that come to mind. Now link one of those colors to how you felt this week or month. Then journal why you felt that way.

1.

2.

3.

4.

Expressing your feelings in a healthy way is important

____
____
____
____
____
____
____
____
____
____
____
____
____

I can have it all

What is your best memory as a child?

15

What is your best memory as a teen?

What is your best memory as an adult?

17

Write a letter to your teen self.

I Love me!
All of me.
No matter
what I've been
through

"We do not learn from experiences. We learn from reflecting on experience"
- John Dewey

18

Think of your worst day, how did you get through it?

Self Love

What does self love mean to you?

1.____

2.____

3.____

4.____

How did you do? Reflect on how you felt doing this and
the thoughts you had.

I
Am
Beautiful

and don't you forget

Self Love

What are some of your personality attributes. Name seven

1.__________________________________

2.__________________________________

3.__________________________________

4.__________________________________

5.__________________________________

6.__________________________________

7.__________________________________

WERE YOU ABLE TO WRITE 7?
YES OR NO
WHY ARE THESE TRAITS
IMPORTANT TO YOU?

Self Love is the best love

What is your biggest struggle loving yourself and why?
When did this start?

Love yourself, Be yourself

My confidence will soar

Miracle Question

If everything in your life was going as planned or "right".
What would that look like?

____
____
____
____
____
____
____
____
____
____
____
____
____

Can you make any changes to get those mentioned above?

____
____
____
____
____
____
____
____
____
____
____
____
____

Goals

1.____

2.____

3.____

4.____

How am I going to achieve these goals?

1.____

2.____

3.____

4.____

Goals are meant to be met

What has been some barriers in achieving your goals in the past?

Are there some changes that need to be made?

I
believe
in
myself

Even if no one else does

Hobbies

What do you like to do for fun?

-
-
-

Have you been doing these things? Yes or No
If no, try to participate in two hobbies this week and
come back and journal how it felt.

____

____

____

____

____

____

____

____

____

____

____

____

1.______________________________
2.______________________________
3.______________________________
4.______________________________
5.______________________________
6.______________________________
7.______________________________
8.______________________________
9.______________________________
10.______________________________

"A day without laughter is a day wasted" - Charlie Chaplin

Describe your ideal partner?

I will not settle

1. ______________________
2. ______________________
3. ______________________
4. ______________________

What can I do about it?

____
____
____
____
____
____
____
____
____
____
____
____
____
____

30

What is something you never told someone?

MY POSSIBILITIES ARE
ENDLESS

Lets check in

How was your self reflection experience?

What is your biggest take away?

Insert your own positive affirmations

" Trust the process."

SELF REFLECTION AND POSITIVE AFFIRMATION

Be sure to follow us on social media to stay up to date with all of our new product releases and blogs!

Filled with Joy 

Naomi Brown | Filled with Joy | www.filledwithjoylc.com

www.ingramcontent.com/pod-product-compliance
Lightning Source LLC
Chambersburg PA
CBHW061530250726
48657CB00005B/2166